THE ENGLISH ASSOCIATION

Pamphlet No. 68

The Northanger Novels

A Footnote to Jane Austen

By

Michael Sadleir

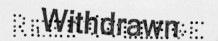
November, 1927

AUTHOR'S NOTE

In its original form this paper was read before the English Association in Westminster School Hall on 11 February 1927. Abridged, and in part re-written, it was published in the *Edinburgh Review* for July 1927. It now appears under the auspices of the English Association once again, but expanded even beyond its original length, and thoroughly revised.

M. S.

Printed in England at the University Press, Oxford
by John Johnson, Printer to the University

THE NORTHANGER NOVELS

A Footnote to Jane Austen.

'When you have finished "Udulpho" ' [said Isabella Thorp] 'we will read "The Italian" together; and I have made out a list of ten or twelve more of the same kind for you.'

'Have you, indeed!' [cried Catherine]. 'How glad I am! What are they all?'

'I will read their names directly—here they are in my pocket-book: "Castle of Wolfenbach," "Clermont," "Mysterious Warnings," "Necromancer of the Black Forest," "Midnight Bell," "Orphan of the Rhine," and "Horrid Mysteries." '

'Are they all horrid? Are you sure they are all horrid?' 'Yes; quite sure.'

TO these few lines from *Northanger Abbey* seven fictions, which would otherwise have faded into complete oblivion, owe a rueful immortality. So long as Jane Austen is read—which will be for as long as there are readers at all—the titles at least of *The Castle of Wolfenbach*, *Clermont*, *The Mysterious Warning*,[1] *The Necromancer or The Tale of the Black Forest*[1], *The Midnight Bell*, *The Orphan of the Rhine*, and *Horrid Mysteries* will survive as tiny stitches in the immense tapestry of English literature. Perhaps such miniature and derisive perpetuity is all that they deserve. But there is at least ground for satisfying oneself on this point by examining the books themselves, so that, having examined them, one may endorse or revise Jane Austen's raillery.

It may be presumptuous to claim for such an investigation that it provides a 'footnote to Jane Austen'. Admittedly—save during its actual pause beneath the Gothic porch of Northanger Abbey— the argument must travel roads which, so far as historical evidence is concerned, Miss Austen herself was content to leave unexplored. And yet it seems probable that the spinster-genius had in her time actually more pleasure and even profit from the Gothic romance than she saw occasion to record; and certainly a woman of her sympathy and perception—however ready she may have been publicly to make fun of the excesses of a prevailing *chic*—would in her heart have given to that *chic* as much credit for its qualities as mockery for its absurdities.

For qualities it had, and good historical and psychological justification also. The Gothic romance was not by any means—as

[1] This is the correct title ; Miss Thorp was inaccurate.

it is nowadays generally regarded—a mere crazy extravagance. Like most artistic movements, it had its primitive incompetence and its over-ripe elaboration; but it sprang from a genuine spiritual impulse, and during its period of florescence produced work of real and permanent beauty.

It is interesting to consider the analogy between the Gothic romantic epoch from (roughly) 1775 to 1815, and the aesthetic romantic epoch from (even more roughly) 1875 to the beginning of the twentieth century. Both of these epochs represented an uprush of the desire for freedom and beauty and, conversely, a reaction from formalism and dignified reserve. By the middle of the eighteenth century the classical enthusiasms, which had in their day been an inspiration to loveliness and had revitalized European taste, had become set. The influences which had once awoken to self-respect and to alertness a culture both flaccid and apathetic, had themselves become a cause of impotence. In its eternal swing from liberty to discipline and back again, the pendulum of taste had reached to the extreme limit of fastidious rigidity. It paused, turned slowly on its tracks and then, swinging ever more rapidly toward luxuriance and freedom once again, swept artists, writers, and political philosophers into the seething excitement of a new romanticism.

And precisely similar was the reaction of the late 'seventies, the 'eighties, and the 'nineties of last century from the controls and prosperous obtuseness of mid-Victorianism. There was more of economic than of artistic arrogance in the last phase of mid-Victorianism; and in consequence more of jealous political discontent and less of pure aesthetic idealism in the rebels of the late nineteenth than in those of the late eighteenth century. But, fundamentally, the two repulsions were alike and, strangely enough, assumed in certain details of their history a very similar guise.

With the political aspect of these movements of reaction the present argument is not (save very casually) concerned. But it is essential to remember, when considering the artistic features of the romantic revivals of the seventeen-seventies and of the eighteen-seventies, that parallel with the experiments of painters, poets, and novelists went experiments of philosophers and political theorists, that—having sprung from dissatisfactions both general and profound—the Gothic romance and the French symbolist movement were in their small way as much an expression of a deep subversive impulse as were the French Revolution itself and the grim gathering of forces for industrial war.

Of the purely artistic manifestations of these century-apart rebellions, it will immediately be observed that, whereas in the eighteenth century the romantic revival affected primarily litera- ture and architecture, in the nineteenth century the arts most ready to take the new infection were literature and painting. The difference is interesting and, as it happens, helps to prove the statement already made that, in contrast to the eighteenth-century movement, that of the nineteenth was economic rather than aesthetic, social rather than philosophical. In 1770, architecture and its at that time important subsidiary, landscape gardening, were still within the province of the artist, who could impose his ideas, subject only to the easily influenced taste of a wealthy and educated patron. But by 1870 the artist had virtually lost control of architectural fashion, having (along with his intelligent Maecenas) been supplanted, on the one hand by speculative builders who built for profit and without other thought than the margin between cost and saleability, on the other by large com- mercial corporations whose taste was not only naturally, but also obstinately bad. Wherefore on the picture-painter of the eighteen- 'seventies devolved the subversive duty of the architect of a hundred years before.

A further significant fact in the tale of these strangely analogous revolts is that both movements began with a return to a wholly fictitious age of chivalry. It is a solemn tribute to the power of legend over history that the undoubted squalors and cruelties of the real dark ages should, by lapse of time and with the help of sentimental visionaries, have been transformed into the shining features of a golden age. What Macpherson's *Ossian*, *The Percy Reliques*, and Hurd's *Letters on Chivalry and Romance* did for the romantics of the eighteenth century, the Pre-Raphaelites, with the *Morte d'Arthur* as their Holy Writ, did for the aesthetics of a century later.

It is difficult to say which of the two enthusiasms was the more admirable in impulse, which the more self-contradictory in practice. Both began as inspirations, both ended as opiates— and opiates against the very same turbulence that they once inspired. Although the neo-chivalry of the eighteenth and the nineteenth centuries was a direct outcome of a fundamental desire for change, or—if you wish—of an instinctive destructionism—it won to wide popularity as a way of escape for minds bored with ordinary life, or, more importantly, for spirits uneasy or terrified before the menace of the future. In other words, the persons who launched the new romanticism were in each century prophets of iconoclasm and yet lived to see the very language of their prophecies turned to the opposite use, to see their once inflammatory art become a drug for harassed minds, a refuge for imaginations in flight from menacing reality.

II

Seeing that the Gothic romantic movement was part of a general reaction against an exhausted classicism; seeing further that, having started as a tonic against restraints, it ended as a drug against a disagreeable actuality, its methods of self-expression were necessarily varied and even contradictory.

But, beneath the multifarious crotchets and pinnacles, with which the Gothic novelist (working side by side with architects from Strawberry Hill via Sheffield Place, Hagley, and Fonthill to the Brighton Pavilion) adorned his fictional fantasies, lay certain general principles of structure and aspiration which give not only a unity to the neo-Gothic movement, but also a logic and a respectability. These principles were related directly to the reaction from classical forms and modes of thought and are interesting as showing what 'classicism' (as opposed to 'Gothicism') meant to the mid-eighteenth century; what conventions and formulae grew up from a determination to evolve an art as *different* from the classical as possible, and how this determination produced a stylized Gothic quite individual to the eighteenth century and not at all—either in proportion or design—a reproduction of a medieval original. In other words, by the way of these principles the student comes at any rate to the threshold of a much-needed investigation—an investigation of those specific qualities of 'Gothistic'[1] art which entitle it to be regarded as an independent style alike in building and in literature.

Perhaps the most striking of the conventions adopted and exploited by these eighteenth-century designers, artists, and writers was the convention of the ruin. This was not in itself a novelty. The classical enthusiasts of the preceding decades had returned from Italy and Greece with so keen an appreciation of the survivals of antiquity that they adorned their parks with miniature Parthenons and set up shattered porticoes on the banks of most unsuitable lakes. But these classical ruin-builders regarded their efforts rather as the modern sightseer regards his diary or his sketch-book. They wanted a memento of the grand tour; they wanted to perpetuate in English meadows the glories of a vanished

[1] This phrase is preferable to 'sham' or 'neogothic', which should be applied rather to Pugin's and, later, to Ruskin's nineteenth-century outbreaks of careful revivalism.

civilization. Consequently their ruins were only ruins because the buildings that inspired them were also in decay; they were not dilapidated for dilapidation's sake.

To the Gothistic eye, however, a ruin was in itself a thing of loveliness—and for interesting reasons. A mouldering building is a parable of the victory of nature over man's handiwork. The grass growing rankly in a once stately courtyard; the ivy creeping over the broken tracery of a once sumptuous window; the glimpse of sky through the fallen roof of a once proud banqueting hall— all of these moved to melancholy pleasure minds which dwelt gladly on the impermanence of human life and effort, which sought on every hand symbols of a pantheist philosophy.

Then again, a ruin expresses the triumph of chaos over order, and the Gothistic movement was, in origin at least, a movement toward freedom and away from the controls of discipline. Creepers and weeds, as year by year they riot over sill and paving-stone, defy a broken despotism; every coping-stone that crashes from a castle-battlement into the undergrowth beneath is a small victory for liberty, a snap of the fingers in the face of autocratic power. Indeed, in these early enthusiasms of the Gothistic pioneers there may be seen with astonishing clearness the impulses that, politically, expressed themselves in the French Revolution. The pastoral chic of the pre-revolution aristocracy in France was another aspect of the same inclination, and there is at once irony and much historic precedent and sequel in the fact that the very folk who thus gave rein to their instinct for revolt lived to suffer, to tremble, or to flee from that instinct's logical development.

And, finally, the appeal of the ruin—as also of the towering crag (another frequent phenomenon of the Gothistic picturesque) —was an appeal of the perpendicular as opposed to the horizontal, alike in structural alinement and in the disposition of shadows. The long lines of classical design, though perpendicular to a certain height, are squared off with the ultimate horizontal of an architrave or with the wide sloping angle of a pediment; the flat surfaces of classical design—whether they be masonry or gaps of shadow—are a part of its style as integral as are columns and projecting cornices. The antithetic pattern in building is one of pinnacles, of fretted surfaces, of intricate broken shadows; and as a basis for such novelty the rebels of the mid-eighteenth century naturally looked to Gothic art and to those aspects of nature, the forest vista and the wooded crag, which were originally the inspiration of Gothic artists.

From this adoption of Gothic forms it was an easy transition to the adoption of similar mental attitudes. The ruin, the bristling silhouette, the flowing untidy lines of piled masonry or creeper-clad rocks became, in terms of emotion, 'sensibility' and an elegant disequilibrium of the spirit. Thus were enthroned alike in visual and in ethical appreciation, ideals of luxuriance, of profuse ornament, and of a rather heady liberty.

Any one who has studied, even superficially, the artistic as opposed to the literary qualities of Gothicism will have noticed how great was the influence of their spiritual origin upon their design and proportion. Houses, churches, pictures, and furniture inspired by the Gothic (or by its easily apprehended twin the 'oriental') mode reveal unmistakably the idea behind their Gothisticism or their orientalism. They exaggerate precisely those elements in the basic styles agreeable to the anti-classicists of the time. In Gothistic examples pinnacles abound; the *ensembles* are thickets of rising lines; the silhouettes are finely serrated. In the matter of curve the ogee, carried out with emphasis and enlarged beyond the normal, dominates the pattern. These and other signs betray the real angle of their creators' approach to traditional Gothic forms; they indicate that, to the Gothicist, the medieval convention of ornament was more intriguing than the structural principles, that—if one may thus express it—the sound of a strange language allured the ear, but its grammar, and indeed much of its meaning, were ignored by minds indifferent to such technicalities.

And in literature was seen an identical phenomenon. Dr. Nathan Drake, the apologist *par excellence* for Gothistic poetry and fiction, is agreeably candid on the point. In his *Literary Hours* (first published in 1798) he says:

> 'The style and poetry of ancient ballads must necessarily, as they were the product of a rude age, be extremely unequal. Though the simplicity, the strokes of character, and description be truly interesting, they are for the most part so strangely intermixed with indecencies and vulgarities as greatly to injure their effect. To remedy this inconvenience, to preserve the dramatic cast and manner of these antique compositions, at the same time avoiding their occasional grossness of diction and sentiment, has been the aim of many modern writers.'

And he proceeds to print two original poems, which he describes respectively as 'an attempt to copy the manner though not the obsolete diction of the ancient ballad', and as 'an endeavour to interest through the medium of Gothic superstition'.

Precisely thus must Batty Langley have justified his Gothistic designs for houses and for garden pavilions; precisely thus must

Middleton have been inspired to recommend 'an elegant fragment of an Abbey for use as a cowshed'; precisely thus must Horace Walpole and Bentley have settled to the embellishment—with furniture, carved woodwork and moulded plaster—of the 'golden gloom' of Strawberry Hill.

III

Of the application to novel-writing of the general principles of Gothistic art much evidence may be found in the seven horrid fictions recommended to the heroine of *Northanger Abbey* by her gushful friend. Within the limits of that brief selection are found three or four distinct 'make-ups', assumed by novelists of the day for the greater popularity of their work. And this fact strengthens the suspicion that Jane Austen's pick of Gothic novels was rather deliberate than random, was made for the stories' rather than for their titles' sake. Chance alone could hardly have achieved so representative a choice; the chooser, had she merely wished to startle by violence or absurdity of title, could have improved without difficulty on more than one of her selection; finally, as we know from her letters, 'Our family are great novel readers and not ashamed of being so', and there is actual evidence that the Steventon household read *The Midnight Bell,* Sydney Owenson's early works, and various other fictions. Wherefore is there good ground for assuming that Miss Austen knew what she was doing when she compiled her seemingly casual list of Northanger Novels.

It is this purposefulness of Jane Austen as satirist of fiction that distinguishes her from her predecessor Sheridan. To quote from *Northanger Abbey* without some reference to the famous novel-reading scene in *The Rivals* is hardly possible; but the analogy between the two superficially so similar episodes is more apparent than real. In Scene II of *The Rivals*, Lydia Languish first receives her maid's report of the vain attempt to obtain a fresh and acceptable supply of novels from the circulating libraries in Bath, and later quickly hides her favourite frivolities, lest she offend the visiting Sir Anthony Absolute. Where Miss Austen's Isabella Thorp mentions six novels, Lydia and her maid mention no less than fifteen.[1] But the moment one attempts a detailed comparison

---

[1] 'Sensibility' novels: *The Reward of Constancy; The Fatal Connexion; The Mistakes of the Heart; The Delicate Distress; The Gordian Knot; The Tears of Sensibility; The Man of Feeling.*

Novels of pseudo-impropriety; *The Memoirs of Lady Woodford; The Memoirs of a Lady of Quality; The Sentimental Journey; The Innocent Adultery; Lord Ainsworth.*

And three of Smollett's novels: *Peregrine Pickle; Humphrey Clinker,* and *Roderick Random.*

between the two lists of titles, their difference becomes evident. Sheridan is concerned merely to satirize the general novel-reading indolence of the young lady of fashion and her secret preference for spice in fiction. Accordingly, in choosing his samples of contemporary fiction, he is deliberately provocative, blending haphazard the vigorous, the suggestive, and the languid, guided by exaggeration of title or genre rather than by subtle varieties in quality of contents. But Jane Austen is more particular in her quarry. She is out after the Gothic Romance, and sets her snares with care and ingenuity.

The Northanger Novels fall into three divisions, of which one is itself subdivisible. *Clermont*, by Regina Maria Roche, first published in 1798, is the rhapsodical sensibility romance in its finest form. *The Castle of Wolfenbach*, *The Mysterious Warning*, *The Orphan of the Rhine* (this is an assumption, but I think a likely one[1]), and *The Midnight Bell* are terror-novels that *pretend*—for fashion's sake —to be translations from the German, but are in fact British-made goods in German fancy dress. *The Necromancer* is of this same class, but with a difference: it probably represents the manipulation of genuine German material to create something to English taste, bearing the same relation to its Teutonic original that the *Englische Sportskleidung*, which filled the Berlin shops in the years before the war, had to the actual shooting and hunting kit worn by English sportsmen—that is to say, the cloth came from Bradford, but the *ensemble* was such as Savile Row had never dreamed of. *Horrid Mysteries* remains—a book not only quite distinct in nature and origin from its fellows, but on a different and higher plane of intrinsic importance and interest. It pretends to be an autobiography; and if it is luridly written in its German original, it has been rendered still more sensational by the mingled guile and incompetence of its translator.

Let us now examine in rather more detail these remote but—of their epoch—so typical romances. Of Regina Roche's novel, *Clermont*, the enthusiast could make a manageable essay, so plentiful is its store of period-ornament, so opulent its rhetoric. It is a pure distillation of what was mistakenly believed to be the essence of Radcliffian fiction. Here is Madeline Clermont, the Gothistic super-heroine, a sort of compendium of the qualities and colours, mental and physical, that were most utterly the mode:

'She was tall and delicately made, nor was the symmetry of her features inferior to that of her bodily form. Her eyes, large and of the

[1] Cf. 'Postscript'.

darkest hazel, ever true to the varying emotions of her soul, languished beneath their long silken lashes with all the softness of sensibility and sparkled with all the fire of animation; her hair, a rich auburn, added luxuriance to her beauty, and by a natural curl, gave an expression of the greatest innocence to her face; the palest blush of health just tinted her dimpled cheek and her mouth, adorned by smiles, appeared like the half-blown rose when moistened with the dews of early morn.'

This entrancing creature lived with a father (over whose past brooded a shadow of mystery) in a charming cottage not far from a 'shattered pile of ruins' in which, after sunset—according to local legend—'horrid noises and still more horrid sights were heard and beheld.' But, of course, 'though feared by superstition,' these ruins were 'the favourite haunt of taste and sensibility', and Madeline spent much of her time wandering about the grass-grown courts or climbing to the broken (but, apparently, still practicable) battlements. From a meeting in this place with an elusive youth of settled melancholy, the adventures of Madeline start on their sensational course. She is taken by an amiable but invalid countess to a distant castle, where she attends routs and makes sylvan excursions, every now and again encountering (and often in the most unlikely places) her mysterious young man, whose name is de Sevignie, and whose occupation is vaguely described as that of an 'officer'.

One night the countess—in the course of an unexplained and seemingly irrational stroll—is savagely attacked by masked men in a ruined chapel in the park. She lingers for a few weeks and dies. Terror now takes possession of the stage. Such a transference from domestic felicity to the dramatics of horror is very characteristic of this type of Gothic romance, and Madeline's escape from the once bounteous and hospitable castle by a secret passage to a grotto; her flight thence from the son-in-law of her late benefactress, who has designs upon her virtue, to Paris where (by the machinations of her persecutor) she is lured into a house of ill-fame; her rescue thence; the lengthy revealing of her father's unhappy secret; her realization of her own noble birth and her ultimate union with de Sevignie, who has at last succeeded in clearing up the mystery of his own identity and emerges as a nobleman of unbounded wealth—compose a narrative than which none is more superbly expressive of the aspiration, the absurdities, but also of the attractive qualities of the Gothic romance.

Mrs. Roche knew precisely the ingredients necessary to fashionable fiction, and blended them with admirable dexterity. A summary of the incidental features of *Clermont* is a summary of the compulsory qualities of Gothic fiction. A low burst of music is the accepted interruption of any reverie in a ruin. De Sevignie carries an oboe wherever he goes and continually 'rivets Madeline to her seat' on a mossy bank or a crumbling stone by the exquisite taste with which he controls the 'soft breathings' of his instrument. Both hero and heroine are 'children of sorrow' (this feature, inherited from 'Werther's Leiden', persists like the Hapsburg nose through the family of Gothic romance), and their mutual sympathy has its origin in a common melancholy. The minor characters include a monk, a comic serving wench, a sinister nobleman with dissolute companions, a sprightly girl friend for the heroine, several elderly countesses, and the necessary peasants, banditti, and retainers. Very characteristic also, alike of the school of fiction to which it belongs and of that school's claim to drug uneasy readers against a painful actuality, is the social background of the tale. Mrs. Roche is careful to give no detailed indication of the date of her narrative, and events of contemporary history, though here and there skilfully implied, are never definitely stated. But the unhampered lives of the nobility, the peasants' submissiveness, and the ease with which persons of quality evade all economic consequences of their very irrational lives, give an impression of the gilded unreality of pre-revolutionary France. *Clermont*, in fact, translates the reader to a vanished paradise of cultured pleasure-seeking where, to those fortunate enough to have been born to wealth and education, all is ease and peace and gaiety. One can understand with what wistful eagerness the elegant but nervous readers of 1798 would follow in this novelist's wake and for a few hours escape the disquietude of fact.

Mrs. Roche was particularly qualified to lull her admirers into a dream of security, because, with all her florid unreality, she had a shrewd sense of social values. *Clermont*, stripped of its Gothic trappings, and when allowance has been made for the modish emotionalism of the time, is really a tale of the day, with characters of recognizable humanity and situations which, exaggeration apart, are not intrinsically improbable. It may be compared with George IV's Pavilion at Brighton, a dignified and normal late-Georgian house, over which has been fitted a shell of tortured oriental ornament.

Finally this authoress can manage incident. Her plots are complex as are those of the twentieth-century thriller, and for the rapid handling of complex plot a definite skill is necessary. Just as the best stories of Mr. Edgar Wallace owe their popularity to the swift manipulation of successive excitements, so Mrs. Roche deserved her public if only for her skill as a sensationalist.

One way to an appreciation of the talent of Regina Roche is to pass from *Clermont* to the two pseudo-German stories by Mrs. Parsons: *The Castle of Wolfenbach* (1793) and *The Mysterious Warning* (1796). These books bear out Professor Oliver Elton's statement that the minor Gothic novelists have no style of their own but a sort of 'group-style', as though they were writing mechanically to pattern and according to models approved and consecrated by public favour. Certainly one may without fear of injustice accuse Mrs. Parsons of the cynicism which gives to the public what the public craves. In others of her books—notably in *Woman as She Should Be* (1793), and in *Women as They Are* (1796), amusing counterparts to the brilliant satires on men, by Robert Bage[1]—she shows a sceptical wit and a capacity for trenchant criticism of her time; but in the 'German Stories' selected by Jane Austen she is too occupied with 'terror' and with Gothistic *décor* to allow herself much realism. Here and there she betrays personal pre-occupations or prejudice. The type of carefully genial hypocrite so surely attracts her when drawing her principal villains, that one suspects an element of actual experience; she is a militant protestant with the strongest disapprobation for Jesuits and for monastic life; above all, her portraiture of mature ladies of the upper-middle class has the sureness of familiarity. But the few passages which betray the authoress' gift for downright if astringent character-fiction are so thronged about with the paraphernalia of a terror novel—with cases of mysterious parentage, with horrid crimes, with 'death embraces', with swoons and pallid gallantry, and with 'children of misfortune' whose lips are sealed by some unhappy secret—that one turns embarrassed from the sight of them, as from bare patches where the basic texture of a well-worn carpet shows through the once luxuriant pile.

Mrs. Parsons' terrorism is further revealed as a mere modishness by her rather contemptuous explanation of all apparently supernatural happenings. Regina Roche, though she did not tolerate actual ghosts, undoubtedly thrilled with her own heroines; but Mrs. Parsons—coldly violent in scenes of almost sadistic cruelty—seems to mock even at herself. Not surprisingly, her habit of giving deliberately trivial interpretations of pseudo-ghostly phenomena robs her romances of their power to terrify, and while she was undoubtedly in herself a woman of much more humour and of better sense than Mrs. Roche, she was very inferior as a Gothic novelist.

[1] *Man as He Is* (1792) and *Hermsprong or Man as He Is Not* (1796).

One further point, before we pass to the other Northanger Novels. The contrast between the work and the personalities of Mrs. Roche and Mrs. Parsons serves to illustrate the difference between the two main schools of Gothic romancers. Of these the first is that of Ann Radcliffe. In mentality essentially English, despite their taste for foreign garb; romantic, but in a friendly bourgeois fashion, the Radcliffians are like persons who sit about a blazing fire on a stormy night. Their sensitiveness to the beauty of the terrific depends less on the actual quality of terror than on the shuddersome but agreeable contrast between the dangers of abroad and the cosy security of home. They listen gleefully to the hurricane without; they even peep between the shutters at the storm or rush into the rain and back again; but all the time they know themselves for safe, and whether they play at running risks of physical catastrophe or of moral degradation, they enjoy the game because it is a game.

Very different is the second school—that of M. G. Lewis, author of *The Monk*. Lewis went to Germany for inspiration and, inverting the roles of fear and rhapsody, used romance as a mere *maquillage* for horror. Into the firelit refuge of the Radcliffian novelist the follower of Lewis would fain intrude, haggard and with water streaming from his lank hair, shrieking, perhaps, as would befit a demon of the storm; then, when he had struck the company to silent fear, he would wish to vanish once again into the howling darkness.

Of these disparate tendencies in Gothicism Mrs. Roche and Mrs. Parsons are adequately typical. The former, indeed, is the principal lieutenant of Mrs. Radcliffe herself. She is an out-and-out sensibility writer, but with a Gothic accent; her own reprobation of crime and terror is as genuine as that of her heroines; she is the direct progenitor of the long and numerous family of story-tellers who have shown innocence and virtue at war with an evil world, but in the end victorious. Mrs. Parsons, on the other hand, is over-cynical for sensibility. She is not so complete a Lewisian novelist as is the author of *Horrid Mysteries* (no British female of the period could have been expected deliberately to shock or stimulate with scenes of fervent fleshliness), but within the limits of her daring and dexterity she does her best. For her, Gothistic mannerism is the candle in the hollow turnip, and one can see her creep (a little clumsily) from tomb to tomb in the shadowy graveyard of her fancy, waiting a chance to bob out at the nervous passer-by and score her tiny triumph. Jane Austen, then, may be given this further credit for her ingenuity in choosing novels for Miss Isabella Thorp—that not only were the fictions of themselves characteristically various, but they represented—and fairly—the two chief tendencies of the prevailing fashion.

The Orphan of the Rhine is the only one of the Northanger Novels of which I am compelled to speak without a reader's knowledge.[1] Long and determined efforts have failed to trace a single copy of the original edition, and the tale was not included in any of the collections of novels issued in cheap periodical form during the 'thirties and 'forties. The book was written by one Eleanor Sleath, and published in 1798. The authoress followed it with *Who's the Murderer? or The Mysteries of the Forest* (1802), *The Bristol Heiress* (1808), and *The Nocturnal Minstrel or The Spirit of the Wood* (1809). One may fairly assume from such a bibliography that Mrs. Sleath was of the Radcliffian school and wrote stories of the approved forest-clad type, staging them wheresoever a likely landscape seemed to offer. There is no reason to suspect her of having translated *The Orphan of the Rhine*, and I have no doubt that, when at last a copy does come to light, we shall find the Rhenish background of the orphan's adventures to be such as might be conjured by a lady of fierce imagination living in Twickenham.

The Midnight Bell, by Francis Lathom is, from the point of view of title, almost a Gothic masterpiece. But unluckily the book itself cannot maintain the standard of its superscription. Indeed it is to be feared that the entitlement was a mere device for penny-catching. The 'Bell' is a signal for the nightly gathering of rascally monks in a ruined castle, where are kept stolen wealth and other improprieties; but it does not toll at all until the middle of the third and last volume, the earlier and major part of the novel being a melodramatic account of the adventures of Alphonsus (good Gothistic name) in search—as usual—of his estates and of the secret of his birth. *The Midnight Bell* is described as 'a German Story', and German in setting and in the nomenclature of its counts and castles it certainly is; but the author was an Englishman and a very witty and ingenious Englishman, although being a person of quality and therefore inclined to idleness, he never worked harder at novel-writing than was necessary to earn a living, and that was not hard enough to do his genuine talents justice.

Lathom began a career of authorship in 1794 with a romance, *The Castle of Ollada*, following it up with a farcical comedy entitled *All in a Bustle*. *The Midnight Bell* was his third work and second romance, and was published anonymously in 1798.[2]

---

[1] Cf. 'Postscript'.

[2] Owing to a faulty attribution of the novel in Watts' *Bibliotheca Britannica* to George Walker, the bookseller-terrormonger, a wrong authorship and a

It would perhaps be unreasonable to quote the quality of Lathom's later work against *The Midnight Bell*; but certainly to any one who comes to it after reading *Men and Manners* (the novel which was published a year later) it is queerly disappointing. Clumsy in construction; humourless and as mechanically a novel of suspense (each of the two first volumes ends with unexplained sensation) as ever was serial in a modern daily paper, the book is like the work of a different person altogether.

As indeed from one point of view it was. Lathom's real talent —like that of Mrs. Parsons—was for contemporary satire; he 'gothicized' half to boil the pot, half to indulge his private sense of humour. Wherefore such books as *Men and Manners* and *Human Beings* (1807) have the light-heartedness of a writer using a natural talent, but the 'tales of terror' from *The Midnight Bell* to *Italian Mysteries* (1820) are cynical exercises in an assumed manner, and wear their trappings with the false solemnity of a knight in armour at a modern costume ball.

Lathom made no secret of his contempt for enthusiasts for the 'mystery' craze among novel-readers (later it became the 'sensation-novel' craze; nowadays it is the craze for 'thrillers'), which he nevertheless exploited with such assiduity and commercial profit. On two occasions he virtually admits that the Gothic romance is to him a mere concession to public taste. Thus, in the preface to *Mystery*, published in 1800, he says: 'Nothing is allowed to please generally which does not excite surprise or horror; the simple walks of nature and probability are now despised . . . In the relation of this story I have endeavoured to enlist in my service those powerful assistants—novelty and mystery.' Seven years later, in an amusing preface to *Human Beings*: 'Trusting', he says, 'that of the numerous novel readers of the present day, an equal proportion at least still retains a relish for what is natural and consistent, I feel no hesitation in quitting the gloomy and terrific tracks of a Radcliffe for the more lively walks of a Burney or a Robinson.'

And there is one further excuse for the imperfections of *The Midnight Bell*. Lathom was new to novel-writing; technique has to be learnt; and the recipe of terror-fiction excluded humour in

wrong date for *The Midnight Bell* has crept into many subsequent records (including Miss Birkhead's otherwise valuable and comprehensive work, *The Tale of Terror: A Study of the Gothic Romance*, London 1921); but later works bearing Lathom's name, the advertisements of his publishers, and one piece of internal evidence show to whom credit (if any) should rightly be given, while an actual copy of the book in its three 12mo volumes is treasured in a collector's library and supplies the date of issue.

favour of a double quantity of horrid incident. The neophyte was at least faithful to his models.

'Arieno was himself the child of sorrow; he had perceived by the dejected air, hesitating speech and pensive mien of Alphonsus that he was a prey to grief equally with himself.'

Again:

'I have learnt from sad experience that the most trivial accidents may carry in their train a complicated and inexplicable string of misery.'

Again:

'I had often indulged similar sensations on spots equally inviting, but they had never produced in me feelings so refined as I that evening felt.'

The only chapters in the novel *The Midnight Bell* that hold the attention of the modern reader (always excepting the few to whom Gothicism is of itself an allurement, who relish even the fatuities of the school) are those describing the imprisonment of Alphonsus in the Bastille and his escape from its walls. These chapters have the realism of fact, and one is tempted to wonder whether Lathom was not actually in Paris during the early stages of the Revolution —a surmise encouraged by the fact that in 1803 he published a translation of a French work describing the transformation of the Tuileries at the hands of the Jacobins.

The Necromancer or The Tale of the Black Forest stands half-way between the sham Teutonism of Mrs. Parsons and Lathom, and the real Teutonism of *Horrid Mysteries*. It is certainly in great part a translation from the German; phrases betray its linguistic origin. But whereas the first edition of 1794 declares the work to be a translation by Peter Teuthold from the original of Lawrence Flammenberg, the records of past German authorship show no trace of any Flammenberg, and the book itself is so formless as to make a single Teutonic original almost unimaginable. More probably it represents an adaptation, according to the English taste, of an anthology of Black Forest legends. This Flammenberg was perhaps an antiquary or even an ingenious bookseller of Freiburg, who had compiled a collection of terrific local tales. From these a selection may have been made, strung together and Englished by Teuthold. With such an origin *The Necromancer* would naturally be what it is, a conglomerate of violent episodes thrown loosely together and not always achieving even a semblance of logical sequence. For magniloquent descriptions of 'horrid' episodes, for sheer stylistic fervour in the handling of the quasi-supernatural, the work can

rank high among its contemporaries; but as a novel it is a failure
and, in likelihood, because in origin it was not a novel at all.

The last—and in some ways the most interesting—of the Northanger Novels is *Horrid Mysteries*. This book, published in 1796,
has authentic German ancestry, being a translation of the so-
called *Memoirs of the Marquis of Grosse* by a German writer Karl
Grosse, who published several works between 1790 and 1800.[1]
His marquisate was apparently self-bestowed, and as an alias he
used sometimes the name 'Marquis of Pharnusa'. Though these
'Memoirs' are beyond doubt mainly fictional, the book has a
strong actuality interest, for it deals at length (resembling in this
Schiller's drama of *The Ghost Seer* and Professor Kramer's novel
Hermann of Unna) with the international intrigues of the sect of
Illuminati, whose savage activities, subversive doctrines, and close
relations with freemasonry are fully described by Mrs. Nesta
Webster in her work, *World Revolution*. To this preoccupation with
the crimes of Spartacus Weishaupt and his followers, *Horrid
Mysteries* owes a second mention in the work of a contemporary
and important author. In Chapter II of Peacock's *Nightmare Abbey*
we read: 'Mr. Glowry slept with *Horrid Mysteries* under his pillow
and dreamed of venerable eleutherarchs and ghastly confederates
holding midnight conventions in subterranean caves.'

The hero of *Horrid Mysteries* falls into the clutches of this secret
society and, because he cannot help himself, swears the oath and
assists at the awful gatherings which diverted the sleeping Glowry.
He learns that the conspirators are political revolutionaries who
decree death to royal persons; that they are social anarchists who
deny all civic responsibility and even the ties of family; that they
believe in communizing alike women and wealth; that they enlist
in their service the knife of the assassin, the terrors of religion, and
the wiles of wanton beauty. Through four volumes the Marquis
of G—— seeks to escape and to destroy the evil conspiracy in which
he is involved. He travels all the countries of Western Europe;
he organizes a Fascist band to oppose the schemes of the Illuminati;
he is continually thwarted by their far-reaching power, brought
back to submission, threatened, made the victim of attempted
murder. The result—in English at least—is a strange wild work,
dealing unashamedly in the supernatural, written with a lurid, if
inconsequent, power. An ultra-Poësque tale of terror, told in
200,000 feverish words and illustrated by Gustave Doré in one of

---

[1] *Erzählungen und Novellen*, 1793–4; *Kleine Novellen*, 1793–5; *Der Dolch*, 1795
(translated into English as *The Dagger*); *Der Blumenkrantz*, 1795–6; *Chlorinde*,
1796; *Liebe und Treue*, 1796; *Spanische Novellen*, 1794–5; *Versuche*, 1798, &c., &c.

his rare but undeniable moments of nightmare genius, would be just such a terrific monstrosity. There is life-story within life-story; the reader seems to assist at a series of apocalyptic visions, which by their sheer opulence of language crush him into gibbering acquiescence. Whatever there may be of folly and even of madness in this extraordinary work, there is also power. *Horrid Mysteries* is surely the most potent *Schauerroman* of them all; certainly in its English version it is the most defiantly fantastic of any novel of the period that I have read.

There is one further element in *Horrid Mysteries* which, because it concerns the Gothic romance as a whole, claims a word of comment. This is the element of voluptuous love-making which, in the opinion of moralists, besmirched many of the productions of the Minerva Press and came in time to be charged (though most unjustly) against the entire school of Gothic romancers. The truth is that, in so far as Gothic romance tended to fleshliness at all, the element appears only in those works which were modelled deliberately on Lewis's *Monk*. And even *The Monk* is to modern taste rather absurd than alarming in its licence. But there were German originals (by which Lewis was influenced) and German successors (in their turn influenced by Lewis) which trespassed further into eroticism than English custom would tolerate. It may, I think, be assumed that of such successors *Horrid Mysteries* went as near as any to the limit allowed to an English translator. The love scenes are luscious and detailed beyond even the aspiration of Monk Lewis himself, and I am aware of no Gothistic novel issued in English during the period that can rival it for enraptured fleshliness.

But one would expect to find in a translation greater abandonment than in a work of purely British origin, and it would be unfair even to the Gothicizers of the decadence to accuse them of following in the footsteps of *Horrid Mysteries*. Certainly passages occur in many English novels published between 1800 and 1820 which suggest that Gothistic 'liberty' might easily have become 'libertine', and that a movement, which appealed to emotion (whether of sympathy, or sensibility, or fear, or love) rather than to reason, could both willingly and logically have drifted into licentiousness. But in actual fact it did not; and the check was not solely due to the social influence (already slowly making itself felt) of Wesley, Wilberforce, and the new puritanism. *La pubibonderie britannique*, often regarded as a Victorian creation, was powerful enough even in 1800 to throw a gauzy cloak of discretion over the antics of novel-writers. Thus national character decreed that the Gothic romance, whence might so easily have sprung a literature of debauchery, should remain this side the border line of decency, and that the occasional trespassers beyond that line should, even in those days, be sent to outlawry.

IV

From the fortunate variety of the Northanger Novels it has been possible to illustrate certain general principles of the Gothic romance. The origins of the movement have been recognized as genuine spiritual origins; the lines along which it developed and the excesses of which it was guilty appear, the former to have been inevitable, the latter—granted the instinct to liberty which inspired the whole—to have been at least logical. It remains to inquire where, when its great days were over, the Gothic romance took refuge; and secondly why, seeing that the Northanger Novels bear—if only indirectly—on Jane Austen's literary experience, they have hitherto only been very cursorily examined.

The posthumous history of the tale of terror is a subject of itself. During the first period of its eclipse—after the historical romance of the Scott type had ousted it from public favour—it fell deep into obscurity and deeper into crude violence and sensationalism. An occasional brilliance—such as *Tales of the Wild and the Wonderful* and de Quincey's *Klosterheim*—lit up, as does a late gleaming star thrown off by a spent rocket, the darkness of its downward rush. But such isolated beauty could not check the rush or break the final fall. The Gothic novel crashed, and became the vulgar 'blood'. But if the once despot of the boudoir became the servant of the chapbook-maker in the slums of Seven Dials; if *The Children of the Abbey*, *The Romance of the Pyrenees*, *The Bravo of Bohemia*, and the rest sank from the drawing-room floor to the sourest recesses of the basement—the spirit of melodrama and of terror (which is only in rousing guise the spirit of escape) persisted unsubdued and persists to this day. Mantalini, the individual, ended his career in a laundry-cellar turning a mangle for a virago; but Mantalini as symbol of male selfishness and of the power of handsome bounders over foolish women will never die. Thus, at any stage between 1820 and 1927 may be found flourishing, in one form or another, the tradition that once was Regina Roche, that now is 'Sapper' and Edgar Wallace. With G. W. M. Reynolds, Wilkie Collins, Miss Braddon, Le Fanu, Ouida, Bram Stoker, Florence Warden, Boothby, Richard Marsh, the list may be extended at discretion. Analyse any one of these sensation fictions, and you will find that it represents precisely that blend of recognizable probability and delicious threatening horror which characterized the romances of the true Gothistic period and gave to them supremacy over educated folk, who certainly knew better but did not care to do so.

As for why this so obvious excursion into the hinterland of Jane Austen has not previously passed beyond the foot hills, the reason is a simple one. The tracks have been obliterated by time; the very whereabouts of three at least of the seven shrines is only by rarest accident discoverable. There are probably no items in the lumber-rooms of forgotten literature more difficult to trace than the minor novels of the late eighteenth century, and for their elusiveness there is good practical cause. During the last quarter of that century the reading of novels became for the first time a widespread fashionable amusement. At once responsible for and consequent on this new diversion was the first great development of the circulating library, which assumed a new and powerful influence among, as Regina Roche might say, 'the leisured fair.' The reading of novels was, of course, held in contempt by persons of serious mind, and retained throughout the period something of the furtive allurement of a secret vice. Actual purchase of novels was for that reason greatly exceptional. A few country houses bought, bound up, and kept the sheet-issues of the fiction-factories; but the bulk of novel-readers sent their confidential maids to Lane's, Lackington's, Hookham's, or Day's to borrow thrills or languishment for their hours of *déshabillé*. From this prevalence of shamefaced novel-borrowing it resulted that the library circulation represented to within a few copies the entire dissemination of an ordinary novel; that the volumes were read to pieces if they were popular, and quickly scrapped if they were not; and that, such fictions being regarded as at best a transient entertainment, it was to no one's interest or satisfaction to care for their survival.

Wherefore the very discovery of texts of most Gothic or sensibility novels is a task beyond the patience of the average student of literature. All but one or two of the Northanger Novels have remained mere names, waiting for some one with the obstinate perseverance to bestow on tracing in one form or another such coy ephemera. And even now, alas, one out of seven is unfound.[1] Who will discover *The Orphan of the Rhine*?

MICHAEL SADLEIR

---

[1] Cf.. Postscript overleaf.

POSTSCRIPT

BY a strange coincidence, the appeal with which the above paper ended has been answered during the actual progress of the essay through the press. *The Orphan of the Rhine* has been found. She is no longer a legend, but a romance in four tangible volumes, published in 1798 by the Minerva Press and over the author's name. It has been amusing to read the work in the light of the prophecies previously made as to its quality and classification, which prophecies—I am relieved to find—were rather true than otherwise. Although it was hardly accurate to assume (as on p. 10 above I have assumed) that the story should rank rather with Mrs. Parsons' novels than with *Clermont*, the guess at its purely English origin, and at its affinity to the Radcliffian school of sensational landscape-fiction staged abroad, is perfectly correct.

Mrs. Sleath stands about midway between Mrs. Roche and Mrs. Parsons. She is more aggressive than the former, with a greater taste for bloodshed and a greater fondness for violent incident; but she is an ardent lover of sensibility, her love-scenes rival those of Mrs. Roche for elegant verbosity, and she takes much greater pains, alike with her character and her landscape-painting, than does Mrs. Parsons.

But perhaps the strongest point of contrast between Mrs. Sleath and the author-translator of *The Mysterious Warning* lies in their religious convictions. The monks and nuns in *The Orphan of the Rhine* (and they are numerous) are all persons of wise and spiritual disposition, which fact, in conjunction with other fragments of internal evidence, strongly suggests that the author herself was a Roman Catholic. Whereas, than Mrs. Parsons no novelist was ever more pugnaciously Protestant.

In matter of *décor* Mrs. Sleath is at once more painstaking and more circumstantial than the author of *Clermont*, and in a wholly different class from the slapdash and conventional Mrs. Parsons. She describes flowers and trees, architecture and furnishings, in considerable technical detail; shows a knowledge of Italian art; and, if one may judge from the adventures on journey of her various characters, had herself actually travelled the country between the Rhine and Salzburg. Some such degree, however, of personal experience apart, she tells a tale of whole-hearted improbability, without indication of period or suggestion of political and social complications, written in true Gothistic language and crowded with episodes of a genuine Gothistic kind. Her orphan heroine, Laurette, and her no less orphan hero, Enrico (their births, of course, are wrapped in mystery) betray the cultivation of their minds by long periods of 'pleasing melancholy'. They are fortunate in having access to a large number of admirable ruins amid whose 'awful desolation' they enjoy several tragical separations, and one rapturous reunion after 'the Orphan' herself has been doomed by a disappointed lover to starve to death in a shattered hunting-box in the middle of a forest. The everyday drawbacks of life under a Gothistic régime are fierce and plentiful. Storms and banditti abound. Hapless victims of oppression are found groaning in dungeons; Italian noblemen have debauched habits but splendid appearance. These and other phenomena keep Laurette and her companions emotionally occupied.

In short, I did Mrs. Sleath no injustice in assuming that her sensationalism would prove rather of the luxuriant and stay-at-home than of the simply realistic kind. She clearly enjoyed herself immensely, on her return from an agreeable foreign tour, in sitting beside an English hearth and releasing all manner of villainy and tempest to rage over the hills and forests of Germany.

The Orphan of the Rhine should, therefore, in the schedule of the Northanger Novels, rank as a Rochian romance rather than as a terror-novel. Judged individually, it is a strangely attractive absurdity, which exercises a sort of sugary fascination over the reader. It may be compared with one of those illuminated waterfalls so popular with organizers of exhibitions. The water cascades over coloured lights, and in so doing offends every instinct of good taste and natural liking on which we pride ourselves. And yet the result is undeniably pretty. As with such a waterfall, so with *The Orphan of the Rhine*. It can be judged artificial and tawdry and absurd; but it is nevertheless pleasant, and one lays down the fourth volume grateful to Mrs. Sleath for her entertainment and ready (as soon as opportunity offers) for *Who's the Murderer? or the Mysteries of the Forest.*

M. S.

FACSIMILE TITLE-PAGES AND BIBLIOGRAPHY

OVERLEAF are reproduced the first edition title-pages of the seven 'Northanger Novels'.

Attention may here be drawn to the fact that, since this paper was sent to press, a complete reissue of the 'Northanger Novels' has been announced by a firm of London publishers (Messrs. Holden) and the first item in the series—*Horrid Mysteries*—actually published.

The editing of this creditable venture is in the hands of the Rev. Montague Summers, who has already written with perceptive scholarship about Ann Radcliffe and to whom, I believe, credit should be given for first declaring that the Northanger Novels were *real* novels and not mere figments of Jane Austen's imagination.

CASTLE OF WOLFENBACH;

A

GERMAN STORY.

IN TWO VOLUMES.

––––––––

By Mrs. PARSONS,
AUTHOR OF
ERRORS OF EDUCATION, MISS MEREDITH, WOMAN AS
SHE SHOULD BE, AND INTRIGUES OF A MORNING.

––––––––

VOL. I.

––––––––

LONDON:

PRINTED FOR WILLIAM LANE,
AT THE
Minerva Press,
LEADENHALL-STREET,
AND SOLD BY E. HARLOW, PALL-MALL.

M.DCC.XCIII.

The *Castle of Wolfenbach* was reprinted in Vol. I of 'The Romancist
and Novelists Library'. London. J. Clements 1839.

CLERMONT.

A TALE.

IN FOUR VOLUMES.

BY

REGINA MARIA ROCHE,

AUTHOR OF THE CHILDREN OF THE ABBEY, &c. &c.

—➤➤●◄◄—

Our Paſſions gone, and reaſon on her throne,
Amaz'd we ſee the miſchiefs we have done :
After a tempeſt, when the winds are laid,
The calm ſea wonders at the wrecks it made.

WALLER.

William   VOL. I.   *Delue*

LONDON:
PRINTED AT THE
Minerva-Preſs,
FOR WILLIAM LANE, LEADENHALL-STREET.
1798.

THE

MYSTERIOUS WARNING,

A GERMAN TALE.

IN FOUR VOLUMES.

BY MRS. PARSONS.

AUTHOR OF

VOLUNTARY EXILE, &c.

---------- " Thus confcience
Can make cowards of us all,"

VOL. I.

LONDON:
PRINTED FOR WILLIAM LANE,
AT THE
Minerva-Prefs,
LEADENHALL-STREET.
M.DCC.XCVI.

THE

NECROMANCER:

OR THE

TALE

OF THE

BLACK FOREST:

FOUNDED ON FACTS:

TRANSLATED FROM THE GERMAN OF

LAWRENCE FLAMMENBERG,

BY PETER TEUTHOLD.

IN TWO VOLUMES.

VOL. I.

LONDON:

PRINTED FOR WILLIAM LANE,

AT THE

𝔐𝔦𝔫𝔢𝔯𝔳𝔞-𝔓𝔯𝔢𝔰𝔰

LEADENHALL-STREET.

M DCC XCIV.

The Necromancer was reprinted in Vol. IV of 'The Romancist and Novelists Library'. London. J. Clements. 1840, where it is described merely as 'from the German' and given as sub-title 'Wolfe the Robber'.

THE

MIDNIGHT BELL,

A GERMAN STORY,

FOUNDED ON INCIDENTS IN REAL LIFE.

IN THREE VOLUMES.

A round unvarniſh'd tale.   OTHELLO.

VOL. I.

LONDON:

PRINTED FOR H. D. SYMONDS, NO. 20, PATER-NOSTER-ROW.

1798.

THE
ORPHAN
OF THE
RHINE.

$\rightarrow\!\!\!\rightarrow\!\!\bullet\!\!\leftarrow\!\!\leftarrow$

A Romance,

IN FOUR VOLUMES.

BY MRS. SLEATH.

Sweet are the uses of adverfity,
Which, like the toad, ugly and venomous,
Wears yet a precious jewel in his head.

SHAKESPEARE.

VOL. I.

LONDON:
PRINTED AT THE
Minerva-Press,
FOR WILLIAM LANE, LEADENHALL-STREET.
1798.

Horrid Mysteries.

A STORY.

FROM THE GERMAN OF THE MARQUIS OF GROSSE.

BY P. WILL.

IN FOUR VOLUMES.

VOL. I.

LONDON:

PRINTED FOR *WILLIAM LANE*, *AT THE*
Minerva-Press,

LEADENHALL-STREET.

M DCC XCVI.

A COPY OF THIS PAMPHLET is supplied to all full members of the Association. They can obtain further copies (price 1s., postage extra) on application to A. V. HOUGHTON, the Secretary of the Association, 4 Buckingham Gate, S.W. 1.

THE FOLLOWING PAMPHLETS issued by the Association are still in print and can be purchased by members. Price 1s. net.

1907–27

OUT OF PRINT

Nos. 1 (Types of English Curricula in Boys' Secondary Schools), 2 (The Teaching of Shakespeare in Secondary Schools), 3 (A Short List of Books on English Literature from the beginning to 1832, for the use of Teachers), 4 (Shelley's View of Poetry, by A. C. Bradley, Litt.D.), 5 (English Literature in Secondary Schools, by J. H. Fowler), 6 (The Teaching of English in Girls' Secondary Schools, by Miss G. Clement), 7 (The Teaching of Shakespeare in Schools), 8 (Types of English Curricula in Girls' Secondary Schools), 9 (Milton and Party, by O. Elton, D.Litt.), 12 (Summary of Examinations in English affecting Schools), 13 (The Impersonal Aspect of Shakespeare's Art, by Sir Sidney Lee, D.Litt.), 14 (Early Stages in the Teaching of English), 16 (The Bearing of English Studies upon the National Life, by C. H. Herford, Litt.D.), 17 (The Teaching of English Composition, by J. H. Fowler), 18 (The Teaching of Literature in French and German Secondary Schools, by Elizabeth Lee), 19 (John Bunyan, by C. H. Firth, LL.D.), 27 (Poetry and Contemporary Speech, by Lascelles Abercrombie), 28 (The Poet and the Artist, and what they can do for us, by G. C. Moore Smith, Litt.D.), 32 (On Concentration and Suggestion in Poetry, by Sir Sidney Colvin, D.Litt.), 33 (School Libraries, by J. H. Fowler), 35 (The Eighteenth Century, by W. P. Ker, LL.D.), 36 (Poetry in the Light of War, by C. F. E. Spurgeon), 39 (The Reaction against Tennyson, by A. C. Bradley, Litt.D.), 43 (The Teaching of English in Schools), 45 (The Greek Strain in English Literature, by John Burnet, F.B.A.), 46 (A Reference Library : English Language and Literature), 47 (The Normality of Shakespeare illustrated in his Treatment of Love and Marriage, by C. H. Herford, Litt.D.), 48 (Don Quixote. Some War-time Reflections on its Character and Influence, by H. J. C. Grierson, LL.D.), 49 (A Note on the Teaching of 'English Language and Literature' with some Suggestions, by R. B. McKerrow, Litt.D.), 50 (The Light Reading of our Ancestors, by the Right Hon. Lord Ernle, M.V.O.), and 57 (Wordsworth's *Prelude*, by the Right Hon. Viscount Grey of Fallodon, K.G.).

Any member having copies to spare of any of the above Pamphlets or of ' Dialogue' by Anthony Hope Dawkins, or of Bulletins Nos. 1, 6, 9, 10, 12, 33, 38, 45, and 49 is requested to communicate with the Secretary, 4 Buckingham Gate, S.W. 1.

Members can obtain further copies of the *Bulletin* (price 6d., postage extra) on application to the Secretary.